Food Aro...

Contents	Page
Pizza from Italy	2-3
Tacos from Mexico	4-5
Sushi from Japan	6-7
Samosas from India	8-9
Pancakes from Holland	10-11
Sandwiches from England	12-13
Hamburgers from America	14-15
Food at home	16

written by Julie Ellis

1

We eat pizza at our place.
To make pizza:
1 Roll out the pizza dough.
2 Put some sauce on.
3 Put the toppings on.
4 Cook the pizza in a hot oven.
5 Cut into pieces.
Now it's ready to eat.

pizza from Italy

At our place we eat tacos.
To make tacos:
1 Cook some meat and beans.
2 Put them into taco shells.
3 Put on some toppings.
They are ready to eat now.

tacos from Mexico

At our home we eat sushi.
To make sushi:
1 Put one piece of nori on a bamboo mat.
2 Put small pieces of fish on some rice.
3 Roll nori around the rice.
4 Cut the roll into small pieces.
It's ready to eat now.

sushi from Japan

At our place we eat samosas.
To make samosas:
1 Cook some pieces of potato.
2 Put spices on the potato.
3 Put the potato on samosa wrapper.
4 Fold the samosas.
5 Place samosas in hot oil to cook.
Now they are ready to eat.

samosas from India

At our place we love to eat pancakes.
To make pancakes:
1 Make pancake batter.
2 Put some batter in a pan to cook.
3 Turn the pancake over to cook.
4 Put some toppings on the pancakes.
They are ready to eat now.

pancakes from Holland

We eat sandwiches at our home.
To make sandwiches:
1 Take two pieces of bread.
2 Put butter on the bread.
3 Put fillings on one piece of bread.
4 Put the second piece of bread on top.
They are ready to eat now.

sandwiches from England

We love to eat hamburgers.
To make hamburgers:
1 Cook some meat.
2 Open a hamburger bun and toast the two pieces.
3 Put meat and fillings on one piece of bun
4 Put the second piece of bun on top.
Now they are ready to eat.

hamburgers from America

shish kebabs from Turkey

What food do you eat at your place? Try a new food from across the world!